Lost and Found
What's That Sound?

Lost and Found
What's That Sound?

LOST AND FOUND

Written by JONATHAN YING
Illustrations by VICTORIA YING

HARPER
An Imprint of HarperCollinsPublishers

Lost and Found, What's That Sound?
Text copyright © 2017 by Jonathan Ying
Illustrations copyright © 2017 by Victoria Ying
All rights reserved. Manufactured in China.

ISBN 978-0-06-238068-5 (trade bdg.)
The artist used Adobe Photoshop to create the digital illustrations for this book.
Typography by Jeanne L. Hogle
17 18 19 20 21 SCP 10 9 8 7 6 5 4 3 2 1

First Edition

For Liz—thanks for finding me.

—J.Y.

I would like to thank my parents for raising me to be creative and follow my dreams and my brother for being an amazing collaborator in life and work.

—V.Y.

Welcome to the Lost and Found,
where we find items by their sound.

The thing I lost goes

Toot!

Toot!

Toot!

I've spent all day in hot pursuit!

Toot!

Toot!

Toot!

That's what I was looking for.

My trumpet! It is lost no more.

The thing I lost goes

DING!

DING!

DING!

Have you heard of such a thing?

My triangle! You found it there!
Thank you kindly, Mr. Hare!

The thing I lost goes

Plink!

Plank!

Plunk!

I play it with my big, long trunk.

My piano! May I have it please?
I need some time to tune the keys.

The thing I lost goes

BOOM!

BOOM!

BOOM!

Have you seen it in this room?

BOOM!

BOOM!

BOOM!

My drum! I see you've found it! Wow!
Just hang on, guys. I'm ready now!

At last I found the Lost and Found!
The things I lost make many sounds, like

Toot Toot
DING

and

Plunk
BOOM

BOOM . . . .

I really need to find them soon!

I hear the things you're looking for.
The sounds are coming from next door!

LOST and FOUND

You found my things! They sound so grand.
One, two, three—